BEFORE DRAGONFLIES

poems by

J Delayne Ryms

Finishing Line Press
Georgetown, Kentucky

BEFORE DRAGONFLIES

Copyright © 2019 by J Delayne Ryms
ISBN 978-1-64662-011-1 First Edition
All rights reserved under International and Pan-American Copyright Conventions. No part of this book may be reproduced in any manner whatsoever without written permission from the publisher, except in the case of brief quotations embodied in critical articles and reviews.

ACKNOWLEDGMENTS

"Certainly Not Another Poetess" first published in Yak Art and Literature, York University, Toronto, ON Canada 1989.

"Narrative Changes" published in The Dry Wells of India, Canadian Poetry Contest 1987-88, edited by George Woodcock, Harbour Publishing 1989, Toronto, ON Canada, 1989.

I would like to thank the continued family support of my mother Delayne Wells, as well as Stan and Janet Barber, Marc and Rejan Barber, and Jorin Ryms. Thanks to those critical readers Sam and Scottie Girgus, Susan Edwards Richmond, Paul Lentz, Sara DeLuca, Pat Butler, Rebecca Watts and the Peachtree City Library Writers Circle.

Publisher: Leah Maines
Editor: Christen Kincaid
Cover Art: Rebecca Watts
Author Photo: Jorin Ryms
Cover Design: Elizabeth Maines McCleavy

Printed in the USA on acid-free paper.
Order online: www.finishinglinepress.com
also available on amazon.com

Author inquiries and mail orders:
Finishing Line Press
P. O. Box 1626
Georgetown, Kentucky 40324
U. S. A.

Table of Contents

"Certainly Not Another Poetess" 1

Narrative Changes 2

Travelers 3

In Limestone 5

Pikaia 6

Arguments 7

Before Dragonflies 8

Nocturnal Horses 10

Lament of the Inarticulate 11

What Saves Us 12

Evolution 13

Cantata of the Wild 14

Anorectic 15

Beyond La Brea 17

The Future of Where We Live 19

Elegy for a Ghost Town 20

In the Plaza Wearing a White Hat 21

The Dead Summer's Soul 22

Absence 23

The Specter 24

Telegram between Betrayal and Forgiveness 26

Dreaming-Horse Time 27

Eohippus Grows Up 28

Linguistics and Logic 29

Love 31

Self-Portrait 32

"CERTAINLY NOT ANOTHER POETESS"
—Robert Lowell

Plath has widowed her words. The
promise of occasion shapes me. What
is monstrous, modest. In the past

I have tended to go too far.
With that assumption I gain ground.
The aesthetic of anger informs
my happening. Parceling myself

like a pie I consume. My twin
makes me vulgar. He is castrated
from this body of thought. The half-
cracked woman gives way. Love details

the wish to become whole, uncompromised.
The wish to please divides. I have
intended to go on

NARRATIVE CHANGES

In the old story, she is able. She can move,
inconspicuously in a roomful of dancers whose steps
are happy. She is everything ordinary and young.

Only the shoes are left, insensible. Visitors arrive
wearing streetclothes, never having spent one day in
distracted isolation. When it all went wrong,

she would remember a day filled with rain, or wind.
Unimportant differences. An afternoon of new distance.
This was not her idea of the scenic route. Ceiling squares,

blood-count. It all adds up to flowered immobility.
A carload of the strictly common, ditched in a country
without maps. After driving to a night of local color,

nothing strange to tell. Autumn across the hillsides,
pastures of bison, the harvest hayride offers typical
testimony. As a woman of character, she enters each dark

with its morphine sense of motion, plotting
impossibilities. Intensive Care: draw the curtain.
She stages a comeback. Tubes for every orifice,

dripping, draining, maintain the body's balance in its
perimeter of bedside equipment. The walls blossom
with Get-Well graffiti. Her feet remember their history,

thrusting back to the dancehall. The crystal globe
spins its splintered light. Memory lodged in nerve-code
breaks loose like a headless hen. When she wakes

alone, the day is bruised, ice-bound. The floor
does not go unnoticed; poppies fall on it,
and a sleepy silence. Even in good weather this is

dangerous. How much of travel is prior arrangement?
A movement toward beds you will make. Name
on the telegram delivered in the dream you plan to have.

TRAVELERS

I have many maps of dreamtime
I'm searching for you in my *EveryWhen*

A theory of loss: old rooms
ghosted
with *nyuidjs*
dust and scattered daylight
        unknowing how
to talk with spirits who roam the place

Of all my dead
you rise
nyuidj
from Aboriginal sleep
your *bardundjari* flying on leg-wings
with *bura*-eyes
               and *bung*-mouth
telling me a way through all landscapes
Time out of Time
        unfathomed in our *dalang*
The Dreaming
fixed and portable

Rainclouds flat and long—
wooden planks making a bridge
between us
              We meet and exchange stones
damara-hand a gesture of friendship
singing the ritual song
              Lightning stones
              To me? give give

I wake as if for the first time without maps, knowing
what was dreamt: the photo of us together in the veil of a waterfall.
You look beautiful, anonymous, but deeply familiar unlike anyone.
What terrains we dared not share with each other. How I explore
the anatomy of words, and you, surgeon-gloved, drive a sapphire car
to the hospital, chart a new cartography of healing.

Blade splits the sternum
Heart sways
in its hammock of ribs, *biba*-crib
      budbut cradled
in maroon-dark
blood
      away from sharp bones
      all the broken *dyaras*

      And wherever we go in the meat/muscle world
is foreign

IN LIMESTONE

Even those who have observed the
sawtooth pattern between emergence and
extinction half agree on a stubborn tendency upward

Turning fossils in Canada, the paleontologist realizes: if this
tree could be replanted
it would probably not result in what we "know"
Several branches of the great white oak end up going nowhere
but given another start they might flourish

Even those who have already charted the
end of the universe comprehend that Cambrian evolutions
recorded and replayed, offer no certainty of sameness

We might see a rather elegant
creature, *Pikaia Gracilens*, worming its sinuous way
upward; we might see it traveling toward some vertebrate conclusion, this
earliest chordate in the Burgess shale
Pikaia swims toward its future in the mountainous upheaval
amid the random bones and shells
The paleontologist reads this ungodly imprint
like a news flash

PIKAIA
For Sam and Scottie

Tentacles
tail-fin
eel-swimming
the jawless chordate
hagfish
570 million years ago
primitive proto-
cord
vertebrate
in the ancient
sea-bed
shale
fish gasping
on the shore to
hunched
mumbling figures who
by slow degrees
stand up
erect
One becomes
the man in a suit
waving his umbrella
bellowing
"Taxi!"
Another becomes
the woman in a field
of grass
and goldenrod
watching the perfection
of horses

ARGUMENTS

Augie March
observes: *if you hold down
one thing, you hold down the adjoining
thing* which may be Heisenberg's
principle of connectedness

In the unscripted wing-flap or dorsal-
flip of evolution
cows are closer to whales than ever
and everything works without the
assumption of god

BEFORE DRAGONFLIES
> ... there is a kind of moth here on the earth
> that feeds only on the tears of horses ...
> —Malena Mörling

Half-dreamt like transparent bones, the moth will feed
at the weeping eyes of Eohippus (a kind of privilege), prethinking
the slim-bodied brilliance
of griffins & damselflies, the conspicuous flight of skippers,
knobbed antennae & the future cliché of hues that
even fossils must forgive.

Lackluster, rice-paper wings on the verge of
whispering, twitch, pull up, thrash against the pane of one
dawn of creation or another, a Pennsylvanian

dusk, Devonian darkness, or this drape of night in a bare-bulb basement,
muffling into sound
or into a substance of unnamed color. Ferning in and out,
Heterocera will fringe its Jurassic
dust on the sill, ghost-trail of premonition,
its encrypted scrawl of reason.
The krill-dripping moon still haunts a Crustacean

twilight, blue-green skimmed from algae, purple

sluiced from asters, silver sliced from mica & from the scales
of lunafish following lotus-stems to the surface, the art
of unlikely unions in the passion

of all plausible elements. Profuse & rank,

these will glaze the netted wing in sun-slick flickerings,
prismatic frays
& accidents of beauty. The leafy wisp of moth
falls fluttering, snatched by urgent

updrafts toward light and back, consumed
with the coming memory of marsh, savanna,
of sun-rippled flanks, brown velvets culled from cattails, dun-yellow
hides from goldenrod,
the sorrels & roans of redclay slip. Prefiguring its butterfly descendants,

the nocturnal moth maps each direction unswayed
by time with drab

iridescence, an echo of itself never-minding in midair pause,
inkling into revision, layered smudges of backtrackings, forgetting,
remembering through which
Eocene creatures cry
& horse toes harden into hooves. Dorsal stripes

develop like a photograph in its fluid, & necks arch upward
with the grace of willows sloping over their creeks,
eyes migrate sidewise like continental drift, & climate taps the
shoulders of equine adaptability.
Panoramic vision grows from wit & willingness as ancient
conifers & giant flora disappear.

Acquiescence waves in
fields of grasses underfoot, foretelling the fetlock,
hock & hoof-trot of the foal,
a kind of Miocene agreement shimmering
in the insect eye, too. A portent of fare slides toward each
alluvial basin, blinked into baptismal
pools, a foretaste of nectar for the moth's alert proboscis, at pace
& canter, the cycle of purpose now

galloping toward its possibilities.

An insect plots to fly, presages the dusty window of
its script, predicts the snuffling muzzle-lips
& brown eyes brimming with the most exquisite tears on earth.
For the first time in history the moth launches itself in metamorphic wingbeats

& pulses toward the horse becoming.

NOCTURNAL HORSES

The season's ill.
Yellow-eyed grass flanks the queasy
hillside; this disease is
lonelier than Tundra ghosts.
My saggy home has slumped a notch, unhinging
the veranda: I'm off my rocking
chair again. The crippled gate sways backward,
groaning dirges to the prairie
smoke and horseweed.

Hyena-wind gnaws at the carcass of the house
and a wretched stench already mourns me.
The blackened, tickseed corpse
is soon exhumed from my romantic
attic, laughing.

Nothing now can cure the nightmare.

My husband, haunted by a shovel,
wraps me in Miss Celie's
color. A talismanic winding sheet is still
no charm for my perfume's
malignancy; nothing warms or now protects me.
Purple linen flaps against my funeral
feet, hooved into granny boots.

I'm sprawled here,
hobbled by the love-me
myth that blooms so mildly
in its cancer.
And all the wild, coltsfooted flowers
mustang my dreaming field.

LAMENT OF THE INARTICULATE
For Dr. Michael Mahaffey

I am the interruption of narrative
                Impulses, comprehension slipping away
From the scene. A wreckage of words.

Casualties, jarring disasters of consciousness,
                Shattered intelligence. I am associative
And disassociative refraction, the ruin of oil in the sea.

I would like to finish a sentence.
                Here is the language for perfect prose,
But infidelities of mind stupefy the air.

I am the horror of fish flopping
                Madly ashore, grease-spot of sun,
Amplified. Talk is a helpless gull in the mire.

Fragments of nouns lie scattered
                On black sand, the coastline of conversation.
All my sorry vowels limp over stones.

I would like to be fluent
                Like the blue dolphins of pure thought,
Slicing in and out of their elements.

WHAT SAVES US
> *We are drowning. All that saves us is love.*
> —Edward Hirsch

Swimming toward my own dormant cries,
vocabulary of water, bass notes.
It means I understand
that I could have touched you.
At the time I thought
I should secret my sounds,
as though my wounded body impedes our music.
I am out of practice, flickering
with messages of bottom-fish and krill, slow
to decode your opera
of fingertips.

If I could describe
this tragedy inside the shark cage, trill
my crusty coloraturas, tell
how I guard my blood to keep its perfume
from spilling—
I could sing my shrill keening
to a soprano you would compose on an ordinary,
sinking piano.

Each morning now I am ready
if you are, trebling off-key to your baroque,
I take you seriously.
As the algae lights shimmer above
I will hold both sides of your whitening face
and tell you that no lover has ever saved me.
Together we will improvise the wail
of rescue boats, emend all codas
of drowning.

EVOLUTION

In the beginning: water.

We're an old rhythm, recurring dream
of male and female.
It's raining as you leave for work.
Spongy and dark, wet-leaf branches at the window.
I lumber to the bathtub, fat from sleep.
The earth drips through me, intent on spring.
New rivers, oceans.

I've borrowed your razor to shave my legs.
Shedding all my seasons today.

Grey light finds the room sunk to my neck.
I splash and roll sideways,
                        changing,
                        righting.
Now in a slow current,
               flowing.

Blue familiar shapes: you're with me.
Warm when I surface.
High clouds move in the trees,
breaking amber.

Tonight I'll glide like the first mammal
between your arms, and nudge you back.
Hundreds of years: our sloping
bodies. Eyes, permeable.

And this will keep beginning.

CANTATA OF THE WILD

This excerpt: Chopin
on the stereo, planks of books, a rocker.
You, bearded with bourbon
and cologne, crawl next to me.
I lay my head in that soft place between
chest and shoulder.
Night dreams like a bloodhound
curled in the corner.

We move together through diatonic
time-zones, improvising a mode
where this could happen.
My world tells me I am too-young twenty,
its injured pet.
Eyes scathe me, hands chafe my hide.
I limp between grief and rage,
looking for refuge.
You, the father friend
who have often named the inarticulate
now discern a woman, blazing
in this cleft.

Beyond candles lit on the hearth,
beyond this secret campfire,
our bodies are mammoth shadows
hieroglyphing the wall.
Tonight in the deep clay caverns, licked
to blue and slick iridescence,
your eyes cling to my mouth.
Night circles the house like a hungry beast
howling our darkness.
You lean into me, pressing deprived air
into pledges against doubt.
I flee, but prowl back dragging
my brute comfort,
its feral breath still on me.

ANORECTIC
For all the perfectly beautiful

in my refusals, I
descend into absolute thinness

dividing down to lowest
denominators in the

lean math of my survival
always elusive

as arrival is departure
& disappearance is no suicide

but a constant vigil
this scant sum of self frozen

in its amber of imperfection
hunger circling

the camp like a furtive beast
keen on the carcass of

plenitude, crouching low on
gaunt haunches

compelled to its terminal
repetitions

the brute shimmers
simplified, eventually vanishes into

unstartled air, like gray fog
into forest, that

last weight of the soul
departing for

wherever we go: apparition,
angel, finally

breaking fast, minus the old
need for calculations,

calories, expenditures, where
the universe subtracts us

according to a measurement
of mass less corpus

on which all perhaps agree
& appetite at last

deserts its function
forgives us our famishments

BEYOND LA BREA
For Susan, who said it

The slippery boardwalk
slides into black tar where lost souls lodge.
Pondfish eyes watch both sides
of tomorrow's time, faint shimmer of something hollow
rising. Swords reflect the moon's
luminous and aloof attachments, its silver
scales of attack, the arc, fullness, and falling. A blinding orb always
follows, its spears of molten gold and goodness
rob the night. Missing its ephemeral target, the last shafts
of fire-forged remorse will pierce the cold again.
The sun's failed ambush hovers
on the horizon like the longing of a lover,
leaving. Prehistoric habits of taking-all
before the giving-back
afflict us, and we are not entitled.

In the metallic aftertaste of public
yawns, I ride my wheelchair ramp to *EveryWhen*.
Translucent as moonstone, a bird screams
with sagging bagpipes, trapped in sticky
blackness. Metaphors flap in murky panic and receding
waves, weary fingerprints of swirled ink.
In glimmers of judgment, the will to think effectively swallows
its cause. Viscous riddles mire me in the pitch
pit between yesterday and yearning
for driftwood. I no longer long for the skill of caulking
canoes like the Chumash.

Mirrors above catch fossil fish.
The bones of sloth haunt me; my domestic dog scoffs.
Ice-age mammals, initially mistaken for horses, pronghorn, even
camels, swam in the asphalt pools,
thrashing and thrashing. Tongvas, too, peopled the swamps, sealed
redwood planks with newmoon glue
into boats. The skeleton of a sole human
recalls its mammoth willingness to fall, the stifling inertia of
not drowning. Coyote trickster, shifty and clever,
surely lured that bird into its sticky
predicament. My world tells
a different story because it cannot imagine such glacial

faults, like missing a rear leg, a vertebra, or the top of a skull.

THE FUTURE OF WHERE WE LIVE
"...*We are in our decadence, we are not entitled.*"
—Amy Clampitt

The bleak, paved-over pastures
hide ancient bones. A pagan woods-god
lures children to
blackberries. The children
carry their own thorns, a legend of quicksand,
husk of corn. Witches will find no kindling.
Fire licks the sugar hills
on the other side where trees grow, always distant.
A wasp stings the Ishi-finger, last
one of a last tribe. RabbitTobacco-spit wraps it.
Automobile smoke occludes
the moon, an orb like the cold stone of an
avocado. The quarry-master in the pit
orders more quartz & granite
because the tall mechanical Man stomps.
Sullen trucks honeybee the
highway. A dim light far away
in the grey sky crackles.
Hornets live in fluorescent gourds left
hanging, & rattlesnake skins coil. The eyes of fish
float in their lakes, always looking.
The quarry heaves rock with
thunder. Its earthquakes unsettle the
ghosts of cows. A mythological bulb of sun lingers
over its ground-up
dirt. There are no more sticks, no more
moccasin flowers
to cover the desolate hole.

ELEGY FOR A GHOST TOWN
For Bruce

Sandia wind gallops endlessly over graves, thieving only sand.
This pueblo, a withered vein in the *Sangre de Cristos*, wrote a funeral
note of placer-gold in pyrite.

Parched trinkets jangle like jaded wind chimes,
season after season, long tarnished. Clouds huff across Precambrian skies
of turquoise. Relics grieve.

Clanking tableware dangles from a skeleton oak. Broken-
hearted spoons & forks remember their
services, clink flat-toned on the wrinkled irony of fishing line.

Golden tells its history on the slope of ancient limestone.
Anasazi prayer-sticks heave up between granite
& Pennsylvanian layers. Spirits sing in the *back of beyond*.

This burial ground, cemetery, offers only its grit,
its rock-ribbed bereavements. Cliffs howl, bereft of ladders, &
the barren wildness reclaims its terrain with echoes.

Pink plastic carnations smother Rosalia Gonzales.
A ceramic swan & faded *flores* for a mother, enshrined.
Someone's abandoned hope of lilies floats in brittle daylight.

Needle cactus & prickly pear scratch the landscape.
Yuccas suck up rootfulls of Catholic bone-dust. *Domingos* bring
Perpetual Care, gifts. A wooden tulip

on a wire stem droops. A babydoll's rubber, decapitated
head stares up. The crazed swan dreams of dazzling lakes.
Kachina and beaded Rain Bird prop against a tiny

gilded church. *Ristras* of cracking pepper-pods hang on the ramshackle,
rotting fence. Scattered red-chile seeds recall Rosalia
and *posole, refritos con* corn *tortillas*.

Only the glass prayer-candles of the saints are missing.
These are what I leave in a windproof ritual, burning novenas for every
soul here that ever petitioned gods & got no answer.

IN THE PLAZA WEARING A WHITE HAT

This *Domingo*, Sunday in mid-spring,
the fruit vendors assembling,
I picture you there
refusing metaphor: fixed in Oaxacan
summer, solstices ago.
I shivered then in the fire of ancestral
prose, a language of missives and
misgivings in which you're more at home.

My eyes are nobody's blue-tiled
patio to the kitchen.
Yours are no dark archway to the Church.
There are no sugar skulls of merriment.
In fact, I'm your street scent of rotting
papaya and mango.

Sometimes in a sharp plaint of daylight,
from the vespers and incense of memory,
brown hands bless me. A soft
tongue and cloak, a lengua not yours,
absolves me.

 The susurrus of *Español*, epistles, your
letters *desconsoladas*
confess me back to our *Mitla*,
our crumbling temple of destruction.
The heat decays every syllable.

All the bones keep dying.
You're my saint-foreign relic, old *cicatriz*
tucked into my pocket. My only salvation is
this ruin of words in a fallen
empire, a sweltering noon that
has long since ceased to matter, some
unholy
        something
        smuggled out.

THE DEAD SUMMER'S SOUL
For Robert

A scent comes with him, his hair. Hardly a blond scent.
High Desert, dry sage. Rio Grande cottonwood and saltgrass
meadow. More than the sweet leaning-into
of a golden retriever, days full of dun leaf-rustlings
and pale, slanting sun.

The mud-sludging ditch where drowned things live,
swift acequia for contradiction, caves
of spiders and bats.
The river itself: placid bogs of quicksand
that sap our fantasies.
But the scent coming with him is clean
and right as a bosque sunflower,

stalk thrusting up in the wrong season.
Cantankerous redwings and rio crows collect
in arguments
and gruff reconciliations—
Hermit-bird merely homes down, ghosting the understory.

He is not mere, this one coming. Nobody's blond scent.
Falling wind. A different sky haunts me
every hour, always vast, exhilarated
by itself expanding. His hair
floats like tall reeds, dandelion tufts, scattered.
The old scent, shimmering.

ABSENCE

Pale mushrooms poke up like ghosts by the amputated
oak. Longing for wholeness.
It was finished, ruined by secondary complications.
Too close to the house.

All the exigencies of
home. Absence, the unintended place, concentric
echoes, abyss of missing. I have seen it in
whirling darkness, whatever the cause.

Dearth, my friend would say, is pain of the arrogant.
What is absence if not longing? The lack of. Wanting.
Wailing. Pleading to go from there before emptiness, before
the hand waving. The voice. —Loss

is the transparency once called something.
Who has not seen the world confused as one who cannot
shed illusions? Distress compels us.
Once there was absence and someone smashed the mirror.

Hands gripped shards. Who understands the
soul of a tree, its yearning? What is natural to live with?
Here is what happened: a woman, of course, saw the one man
she loved, dependable, somewhere else.

In the dead of winter soil froze around the stump.
We can die many times. The woman lived with her desire,
her need to cut something, her need
to be cut. Wait, it doesn't end there. The photo-grins

hissed, curled up in flames, typical of stories
like this. She was a victim of burning
illusions & she knew it. Or take it from his perspective: he
was dependable. He stayed. But one cannot live in moldering

absence, so he left her in her own house.

THE SPECTER

One month after your funeral I dreamt you back to us,
mute, mouth sewn shut like the cadaver
in the coffin between rose-pink torchiers at the funeral home.

Awake, terribly wrong, but right, as if this
always happens to the dead, you slumped there, waiting for
your own memorial service to begin, as we all waited.

Longing and loath to touch you, I bent toward your plump
husk *Are you ok? Do you need some help?*
But you just sat there, undead, unresponsive as you were

in your last few hospital days. Then you rose with selfless difficulty,
shuffling slowly, as that night toward the bathroom and the fall
from which you would not recover.

You heaved up, head high, lurching
between my questions. I leaned near, calling, still mortified
to touch your corpse. Recoiling from its bloodless skin, I pleaded

Can I help you? to your blank, impassive face.
In sutured dream-time you acquired a walker, pivoted behind me
in your mindless trek. You will be my

crewelpoint-macabre, waiting, pacing, lips
stitched against a swollen tongue, eyes open in a blue-grey
fog of incognizance, unaware of all but this delay,

innocent of lingering here without spirit or voice, words swallowed
in a muscle-fugue. The grave affliction of unrest
haunts embalmed flesh. You were the griefless trance

of memory roused from sleep, waking care in me.
You *are* the unspeakable. It is that last embroidery of silence
that scares me, when the needle-hook of thread is cut.

When that last tatting of eulogies and crying
over coffins is over, we will carry the ghastly apprehension
that the dead cannot be helped, that we

must bear the staggering weight of their absence.

TELEGRAM BETWEEN BETRAYAL AND FORGIVENESS

I orphan myself
rip out the primitive worm of badness
twisted back on itself through the good skin,
past the point of shrift. Heave it growling like a catamount
over the Rio Gorge, thudding against granite,
a long, unfaithful throw, grinding the flesh of the skull
away when I need it most to be wide-eyed alive,
a willing culpability.

I console myself
cave-sign apologies, red ochre handprint to the sullen one
who scorns me now. My crime hangs
like a bat. Entreat the other half of the fractured
lifeline, my dubious palm to hers, she who mopes
from our molten past over Cretaceous
limestone and shale, dividing our futures on a fault, I fall
marooned by remorse, self-recriminations.

      Has anyone seen it, thumping against volcanic
      crust and sharp rocks, flopping in panicked air like a cutthroat
      or spinning like a falcon, feathers smashed in sticky
      clumps? Stop. Has anyone seen my bruised and broken ghost
      with a map, the field guide back from this blood river?

DREAMING-HORSE TIME

The frozen bones of Tundra
ponies recollect themselves in my Siberia,
not yet imagining their progeny. The Yana mammoth's
dreams lie barren as panic wakes the valley.

Displaced Asian stallions and diluvial dams
have foaled a herd behind my frantic
eyelids. The heavy-headed, dappled hybrids
wander off from history, burdened by my frightful

hindsight. Steppe bloods graze on alone,
bristling upright manes, but massive forest brutes,
foretelling drays and dobbin-cobs for cargo,
bog down in wooded swamps.

Tarpans trick what's left of dun plateaus,
ghost themselves like deer for present Polish winters.
Dorsal stripes and high, pre-Caspian tails
swift past their Arab future.

The climate in my skull grows colder, glacial,
nips at the feral brood
to fend off old, impending blizzards.
No matter that the recent clocks are cuckoo

in my snoozing bedroom. Equine time's
askew: all the hippus primitives defy chronology.
I join in midnight exile my romantic,
fetlocked fossils, a skittish pack of passions

galloping toward the brink.
And now, my leggy antecedents stampede me
back to Eocene epiphanies, back to the blue heat
and river fog of poetry.

EOHIPPUS GROWS UP

                         In a swaybacked play
of 60-million years,
foreshadowing African, eel-striped cousins
and domestic asses in my Americas. The matriarchal
Eo-horse, no bigger than a fox,
trots figuratively through Geo-logic,
revising equine eyes at each impressionable
stage for more dramatic panorama.

                        She's a pre-modern
metaphor in dappled motion, the plot's aptly
improvisational. The weight of apple-loving,
alliterated heirs speeds her surefooted art
for all the ages, while literary sugar lumps clog
the local bogs with fossils.
                               Prototypically growing
heavier on the stressful journey, she spondees
to accentuate her fitness. Eyes still migrate sidewise
like continental shift. She thrusts out her trochaic
neck for better browsing and a long, iambic
look beyond the landbridge.
                          In the mud-marsh trek
to dry savanna, she loses squishy,
primal toes, reinvents herself, emphatically with hooves,
for leaping all the fallen
analogies.

LINGUISTICS AND LOGIC
For A-jorin

I watch my son stand on his
red chair at the sink, pour from one unbreakable cup
to another, exploring over and over
the properties of water.

I Spanish him with *poesia*, susurrate
what could otherwise not be said with glottals,
though he's not impressed by fantasy or
foreign words,
grappling with *this, what is*, one-syllable mouthfuls,
contraptions disassembled, tried again
and again, the full facts of *his* world
hammered to happy invention and pulled apart once more
by the genius of being two.

In his way, I study our accumulated time, its ripples, repetitions, tautologies,
      what is not mellifluous or brilliant,
in waves of seeing, breaking,
retreating back to the same Germanic shore, only different by degrees of light and
weather, each pulse bringing in and taking back its gifts:
      seaweed debris, cracked shells, and shipwreck, colloquial

bits of bottle-glass worn smooth, pastel (noting
dullness rather than color). I delve into vessels that have traveled here
fraught with unsinkable losses.
The fragments I cull more fully, learning the weight of
what is absent, the trip's epic
      imperfections.

Is it possible to grasp the completeness of something
by what is missing?
No matter what eddies in, we take and return it, transmute
the bliss or pain of it, and
perhaps mosaic the opaque shards, what is
      discarded, picked up, reconfigured by

the work of being human, this luminous
tumbling of the *so on* and *so on*, into the
soon, soon,
until it is, today, this labor, delirious in detail,
sufficient, the cup held out: "drink?"
a child proffering the tangible thing, a durable kindness
that deconstructs the heart and changes
everything.

LOVE
After Joy

Now I writhe from crackling coils of skin, see
how I slough off old parchment, the bandaged face,
my own husk of boredoms, a cicatrix,
this bloodspot of charred responsibility, this scar
of a woman-corpse married to its
destinations, ash and mud wrinkling my soles.

Now I stagger from the fire, from molten earth, see
how I rise in seared agony, dragging that teardrop at the end
of our sentences, a black-muzzled minute,
the haunted look in equine eyes,
your brow furrowed in mid-air like a letter asking
something in a rasp of language I will never comprehend.

Now I let this shadow of green be a fiddlehead gesture, see
how untold, curled-up longing
unfolds, embellishes itself on my lips, hair, eyelashes,
leaves its ghostly evidence like words on scorched paper,
like vanishing ferns, the galloping persistence of cave-horses,
or the whispers of ice on your fingers.

Now I cradle you, wounded, dazed, not entirely drained
of blood and bravery I don't believe in anymore.

SELF-PORTRAIT

Lifted out of the high chair,
crawling, baby-block of alphabet
cupped in each hand,
I toss my head, stamp linoleum,
sprout forelegs, hocks, black hooves.

        Mute, Moorish
        as the animal I am, poised
        to interpret wind
        olive moon in esparto grass
        I translate the pine-smoke embers
        of far-away fires
        sky of herbs and rain soon

Now fixed in a metal chair, on wheels,
knowledge of me imagines pain,
like the spine crunching hard against
car-steel, bloodstained
glass, everything that shatters.

        I run
        long lifetimes to keep beyond them
        Autumn flanks the hillside
        dun, chestnut
        wind-snort and thunder
        I breathe the proximity of horses
        buckskin, muscling hides,
        bays and blue roans
        The staccato of drumming behind me
        beats on my heart with a
        stutter of hooves and a song
        I cry back to it
        beyond canyon and lake
        over wind, over prairie
        Surely someone must know what I've been
        struggling to say
        and never having said, I
        run on

NOTES

"*Travelers*" uses terms and concepts humbly borrowed from Australian Aboriginal beliefs and mythology, such as "time out of time" or "Everywhen," during which the land was inhabited by ancestral figures. "Nyuidj" refers to a dead spirit in the Wangga genre. "Bhardunjari" is also spirit. "Bura" means testicle; "dalang" is tongue; "danara" hand; "budbut" heart; "biba" rib; "dyara" bone; "bung" stopper for a cask.

"*In Limestone*" refers to an ancient worm-like species, Pikaia Gracilens, from Cambrian geotime that left its imprint in an ocean floor (now the Burgess Shale near Banff, Canada). Pikaia's phenotype suggests to some paleontologists that it may be humankind's oldest known ancestor, one of the most primitive vertebrates.

"*Dreaming-Horse Time*" refers to four primitive horses, considered virtually extinct: Tundra Pony discovered in the Yana Valley, Siberia with mammoths; Przwalski's Horse found in the Asian Steppes shares the trait of an upright mane with Zebras; Forest Horse from European swamps, ancestor of draft horses; Tarpan, small, tan with dorsal stripe and arched tail, camouflaged itself in winter snow with a white coat, precursor of the modern Arabian horse.

"*Elegy For A Ghost Town*" refers to Golden, a mining town in New Mexico first inhabited by Native Americans and Spaniards before the gold discovery in 1825. Anasazi, or Old Ones/ancestral Pueblo Peoples, a culture that populated the Early Basketmaker II Era, best known for their enduring apartment-style villages such as still-inhabited Taos Pueblo.

J **Delayne Ryms** earned a Master's degree from the University of California at Davis. Her poetry has appeared in various journals and anthologies such as *The Comstock Review, High Plains Literary Review, Puerto Del Sol, Looking for Home (Milkweed Editions), Frontier Poetry,* and *Wild Apples, a Journal of Art and Inquiry.* Her poetry has appeared in local writing-guild anthologies, earning publications in *Rhythm and Rhyme*, an annual poetry contest/anthology sponsored by the Peachtree City Library. Her work has received numerous awards, including a grant in literature from the California Arts Council; *Dreams, Art, & Archetypes* poetry award; an interdisciplinary prize in art and literature; a prize and publication from The Canadian Poetry Contest; nomination for a Pushcart Prize; and two Academy of American Poets Awards. A collection of her poetry was selected as a finalist in Nimrod's Pablo Neruda Contest. She lives in Georgia with son Jorin and service dog Kai. She is a volunteer writer for the collaborative organizations of local animal rescue Coco's Cupboard, professional training services TAO K9 Unleashed, and Healing4Heroes which provides service dogs to disabled veterans.

www.ingramcontent.com/pod-product-compliance
Lightning Source LLC
LaVergne TN
LVHW041559070426
835507LV00011B/1199